STREET
FOOD
— OF INDIA —

STREET FOOD

FOOD

— OF INDIA —

Lustre Press
Roli Books

Published in India by Roli Books
M-75, Greater Kailash II Market
New Delhi-110 048, India
Ph: ++91-11-40682000
E-mail: info@rolibooks.com
Website: www.rolibooks.com

Cover design: Adviata Vats
Editor: Priya Kapoor, Saachi Khurana
Layout design: Bhagirath Kumar

ISBN: 978-81-937501-4-8

CONTENTS

Bonda	39
Dhuska	40
Fried Garadu	41
Besan Ka Chila	42
Methi Thepla	43
Aloo Kabli	44
Chura Mattar	45
Pao Bhaji	46
Amritsari Kulcha	48
Bhelpuri	50
Spicy Dahi Vadas, South Indian Style	52
Litti Chokha	54
Masala Dosa	56

NON-VEGETARIAN

Aamlette	59
Mutton Seekh Kebab	60
Tandoori Chicken	61
Amritsari Macchi	62
Murgi Minced Cutlets	63
Mangsho Ghugni	64
Lukmi	65
Egg Banjo	66
Maacher Chop	67
Mangsho Cutlet	68
Chingri Cutlet	69
Shammi Kebab	70
Momo	72
Chilli Chicken	74
Chicken Kathi Roll	76

DESSERTS

Gajar Ka Halwa	79
Kulfi Falooda	80
Jalebi	81
Gulab Jamun	82
Shahi Tukda	83
Besan Ladoo	84
Payasam	85
Gajak	86
Mishti Doi	87

DRINKS

INTRODUCTION

It is said that the spirit of a place resides in its streets. This is evidenced by the splendour of the veritable melting pot called India, which comes alive amidst vibrant scenes of bustling bazaars, teeming corners and crowded alleys. Inevitably, even a cursory understanding of India's complex culinary heritage requires a familiarization with the hidden specialties tucked away in its circuitous lanes and bylanes.

Indian street food is as astoundingly heterogeneous as its cultural landscape, and the intermingling aromas wafting through the air of the streets can be overwhelming at first encounter. This book captures such Indian peculiarities by bringing together authentic food like Jhal Muri from West Bengal and spicy Dahi Vada from South India. It is a cohesive compilation of over 70 specially curated recipes, which include popular and much-loved dishes besides lesser-known delicacies.

Street Food navigates the delightfully variegated experience that Indian street food offers. In doing so, it brings to life little-known dishes like the lip-smacking Hyderabadi Lukmi, as well as popular street foods like the buttery Maharashtrian Pao Bhaji. The Drinks section comprises a number of refreshing beverages to quench your thirst on a hot summer day. One can also find recipes of Indian variations of global snacks, like Chow Mein, Mumbai Vegetable Sandwich and 'Aamlette'.

The mouth-watering culinary trail charted by *Street Food* will certainly leave you hungry for more!

VEGETARIAN

VADA PAO
Indian-style potato burger

• Ingredients •

- → 4 medium-size potatoes, boiled, peeled, mashed

- → 2 cups (240 g) chickpea flour (*besan*)

- → Salt, to taste

- → 1 tsp turmeric (*haldi*) powder

- → 2 garlic cloves

- → 1 in. ginger

- → 1 cup (16 g) green coriander (*hara dhaniya*), chopped

- → 2 medium-size onions, chopped

- → Vegetable oil, for deep-frying

- → Bread rolls (*pao*)

• Method •

1 In a large bowl, combine the chickpea flour, turmeric powder and salt. Mix well. Add enough water to make a batter of medium-thick consistency.

2 In a food processor or with a pestle and mortar, grind the garlic and ginger to make a paste. Add the mashed potatoes, green coriander and onions. Mix well.

3 Divide the mixture equally into 6 small dumplings.

4 In a wok over medium heat, heat the vegetable oil. Deep-fry the dumplings till golden brown.

5 Now coat the dumplings with the chickpea flour batter and fry again till golden brown. Remove and drain on paper towels.

6 Split the bread rolls into half, keeping the base intact. Place the dumplings inside and serve with your favourite chutneys.

KHASTA KACHORI
Spicy dal-stuffed kachori

• Ingredients •

→ 1 cup (200 g) split yellow gram (*moong dhuli*), boiled

→ 1 cup (200 g) split black gram (*dhuli urad dal*), boiled

→ 3 green chillies, finely chopped

→ 2 Tbsp (30 g) ginger-garlic (*adrak-lasan*) paste

→ 2 tsp dried mango powder (*amchoor*)

→ 1 Tbsp (6 g) ground coriander (*dhaniya*)

→ 1 tsp fennel (*saunf*) seeds

→ 1 tsp ground turmeric (*haldi*)

→ 1 tsp garam masala

→ 1 tsp ground cumin (*jeera*)

→ Salt, to taste

→ 1½ cups (188 g) whole-wheat flour (*atta*)

→ Water, for kneading

→ Oil, for frying

• Method •

1 In a medium-size bowl, combine the split yellow gram, split black gram, green chillies, ginger-garlic paste, dried mango powder, coriander, fennel seeds, turmeric, garam masala, and cumin. Mash together slightly and season to taste with salt. Set aside.

2 In a medium-size bowl, combine the whole-wheat flour with just enough water to knead the dough. Divide the dough into 10 small balls and roll them out into small discs, about the size of your palm.

Place a spoonful of filling at the centre of each disc and bring all the edges together.

3 In a deep skillet over medium-high heat, heat the vegetable oil for frying.

4 Carefully add the stuffed fritters (kachoris) to the hot oil and deep-fry until golden. Serve with your favourite chutneys, if desired.

PAKORA
Vegetable fritters

• Ingredients •

- → 1 large potato, peeled, sliced
- → 1 medium-size aubergine (*baigan*), sliced
- → 1 large onion, sliced

For the batter:

- → 2 cups (240 g) chickpea flour (*besan*)
- → Salt, to taste
- → 1 tsp red chilli powder
- → ½ tsp baking powder
- → Vegetable oil, for frying

• Method •

1 In a bowl, combine all the ingredients for the batter. Mix well, adding a little water to make a very thick batter.

2 In a wok over low-medium heat, heat the vegetable oil. One at a time, dip the sliced vegetables into the batter. Deep-fry until crisp and golden brown. Remove with a slotted spoon and drain on paper towels.

3 Serve hot with your favourite chutneys.

SAMOSA

Triangular vegetable patties

• Ingredients •

- → 1 Tbsp (15 ml) vegetable oil, plus more for deep-frying
- → 1 tsp cumin (*jeera*) seeds
- → 2 green chillies, finely chopped
- → 1 tsp ginger paste
- → 1 tsp ground turmeric (*haldi*)
- → 1 tsp red chilli powder
- → 2 cups (450 g) potatoes, mashed

- → 2 tsp garam masala
- → 1 tsp chaat masala
- → Juice of 1 lemon
- → ¼ cup (4 g) green coriander (*hara dhaniya*) leaves
- → Salt, to taste
- → 1 package samosa pastry sheets (*samosa patti*)
- → Vegetable oil, for frying

• Method •

1 In a skillet over medium-high heat, heat 1 Tbsp of vegetable oil. Add the cumin seeds. Cook until the seeds begin to crackle.

2 Add the green chillies, ginger paste, turmeric, and red chilli powder. Stir well to combine.

3 Add the mashed potatoes, garam masala, chaat masala, lemon juice, and coriander. Season to taste with salt. Mix well. Set aside.

4 Place a spoonful of the mixture on a samosa pastry sheet and wrap to enclose it in a triangular shape. Repeat until all filling and pastry are used up.

5 In a wok over medium-high heat, heat the vegetable oil for deep-frying. Working in batches if needed, carefully add the stuffed samosas to the hot oil and deep-fry until golden. Transfer to paper towels to drain.

6 Serve hot with your favourite chutneys.

SADA KULCHA

Plain baked bread

• Ingredients •

- → 1 cup (240 ml) milk
- → 1 tsp sugar
- → 3 tsp yeast
- → 4 cups (500 g) refined flour (*maida*)
- → 1 tsp salt

- → 1 Tbsp (15 ml) ghee
- → 4 Tbsp (60 g) yoghurt (*dahi*)
- → ½ cup (120 ml) water
- → 2 Tbsp (18 g) poppy seeds (*khus khus*)

• Method •

1 In a pan over low-medium heat, warm the milk. Add the sugar and yeast. Remove and leave aside for 20 minutes.

2 In a large bowl, sift the flour with the salt. Pour in the milk and yeast mixture along with the ghee. Mix well. Slowly add the yoghurt and knead into a soft dough. Cover with a damp cloth and leave aside for 6 hours.

3 Knead well again, if required, and add a little warm water. Divide the dough into 10 lemon-size portions and roll them out into thick discs of 5 in. diameter. Place them on a baking tray. Cover with a damp cloth for another 30 minutes to rise.

4 Brush the top of each disc (kulcha) with a little milk or ghee and sprinkle with poppy seeds.

5 Preheat the oven for 10 minutes on 180°C (350°F). Bake the kulchas for 10 minutes until golden brown on both sides. Serve with chhole (p. 16).

15

CHHOLE

SERVES 2

Spicy chickpea curry

• Ingredients •

- → 1 cup (200 g) chickpeas (*kabuli chana*), soaked in water

- → 3 cups (720 ml) water

- → 1 teabag or 1 tsp tea dust wrapped in muslin cloth

- → 1 Tbsp (15 g) whole spice mix

- → 1 Tbsp (6 g) ground coriander (*dhaniya*)

- → 2 dried red chillies (*sookhi lal mirch*)

- → 1 Tbsp (15 g) ginger-garlic (*adrak-lasan*) paste

- → Salt, to taste

- → Juice of 1 lemon

- → 1 tsp fennel (*saunf*) seeds

- → 1 Tbsp (15 ml) vegetable oil

- → 1 tsp cumin (*jeera*) seeds

- → ¼ cup (43 g) onions, finely chopped

- → 1 medium-size green chilli, finely chopped

• Method •

1 In a pressure cooker, combine the drained chickpeas with 2 cups water and teabag or tea dust wrapped in muslin cloth for 10 minutes or until soft. Drain and reserve the water.

2 Once cool, mash gently with a potato masher. Add the lemon juice and fennel seeds. Mix well and set aside.

3 In a skillet over medium-high heat, heat the vegetable oil. Add the cumin seeds. Cook until the seeds begin to crackle. Add the onions and green chilli. Sauté for 1–2 minutes.

4 Add the mashed chickpea mixture. Mix well. Reduce the heat to low and simmer for 7–10 minutes. Serve hot with kulcha or bhature (p. 17).

BHATURE
Deep-fried leavened bread

• Ingredients •

→ 2 cups (250 g) refined flour (*maida*)

→ ½ tsp soda bicarbonate

→ Pinch salt

→ 1 tsp sugar

→ 4 Tbsp (60 g) yoghurt (*dahi*)

→ 5–6 Tbsp (75–90 ml) water, warm

→ 1 tsp ghee, melted

→ Vegetable oil, for deep-frying

• Method •

1 In a large bowl, mix the refined flour with soda bicarbonate and salt and sieve it all together.

2 Add sugar, yoghurt and enough warm water to knead into a smooth dough. Knead till the dough stops sticking to your fingers or to the sides of the bowl. Grease your palms with 1 tsp ghee and continue to knead till the dough becomes pliable. Cover with a damp cloth and set aside in a warm place or over a pan of warm water for 4 hours.

3 Divide the dough into 10 equal parts; shape into balls and roll out discs with 4 in. diameter. Keep them covered on a tray.

4 In a wok over low-medium heat, heat the vegetable oil. Deep-fry the discs, one at a time, till they puff up and turn light golden. Remove with a slotted spoon and drain on paper towels. Serve with chhole (p. 16).

CHOW MEIN
Vegetable noodles — Indian style

• Ingredients •

→ 1 packet (200 g) noodles (egg noodles or vegetable noodles)

→ 2 Tbsp (30 ml) vegetable oil

→ 1 medium-size onion, finely sliced

→ 2 green chillies, chopped

→ 1 medium-size capsicum, sliced

→ 1 medium-size cabbage, shredded

→ 1 medium-size carrot, sliced

→ ½ cup (50 g) green beans, chopped

→ 2 Tbsp (30 ml) soya sauce

→ 2 Tbsp (30 ml) vinegar

→ Chilli sauce, to taste

→ Salt, to taste

→ Water, as needed

• Method •

1 In a pan, boil the noodles in enough water till soft but not overcooked. Rinse the noodles 2–3 times in cold water; drain and set aside. Add a few drops of oil to the noodles to avoid sticking.

2 In a wok over low-medium heat, heat the vegetable oil. Add the onion and green chillies and stir-fry for 20–30 seconds. Add the capsicum, cabbage, carrot and green beans and stir-fry for 2 minutes. Add salt and mix well.

3 Add the boiled noodles and mix well (taking care that the noodles don't break). Now add soya sauce, vinegar, and chilli sauce; stir-fry for a minute.

4 Serve hot.

JHAL MURI
Seasoned puffed rice

• Ingredients •

- → 1 cup (240 g) puffed rice (*murmura*, available at grocery stores)

- → 1 small onion, finely chopped

- → 1 small potato, boiled, peeled, finely chopped

- → 1 Tbsp (30 g) tomatoes, finely chopped

- → 1 Tbsp (30 g) cucumber, finely chopped

- → 2 tsp ginger, finely chopped

- → 2 green chillies, finely chopped

- → 2 Tbsp (18 g) peanuts, fried

- → 2 tsp sprouted black gram (*kala chana*), soaked in water, drained

- → 4 tsp mustard (*rai*) oil

- → Salt, to taste

• Method •

1 In a large bowl, combine all the ingredients except the mustard oil and salt. Mix gently with a fork.

2 Add the mustard oil and salt. Mix gently again.

3 Serve as a snack at tea-time.

IDLI
Savoury rice cake

• Ingredients •

- 1 cup (200 g) idli rice, soaked in water for 6 hours, drained

- ¾ cup (150 g) split black gram (*dhuli urad dal*), soaked in water for 6 hours, drained

- Water, as needed

- ¼ cup (4 g) green coriander (*hara dhaniya*) leaves, finely chopped

- 1 tsp ground turmeric (*haldi*)

- Pinch ground asafoetida (*hing*)

- 1 Tbsp (15 g) ghee

- 5 curry leaves (*kadhi patta*)

- 1 Tbsp (13 g) split Bengal gram (*chana dal*)

- 1 Tbsp (15 g) ginger-chilli (*adrak-mirch*) paste

- 1 tsp cumin (*jeera*) seeds

- 1 tsp mustard (*rai*) seeds

- Salt, to taste

• Method •

1 In a food processor, combine the rice and split black gram. Grind together into a coarse paste.

2 Add water to adjust the consistency, making it not too thick or thin, simply pourable. Cover and let ferment at room temperature overnight.

3 Whisk the rice and black gram mixture and add the green coriander, turmeric, and asafoetida. Stir well to combine.

4 In a skillet over low-medium heat, heat the ghee. Add the remaining ingredients. Cook until the seeds begin to crackle. Add the mixture to the batter.

5 Stir well. Fill an idli mould with the batter.

6 Steam for 10–12 minutes and serve hot with *sambhar* and your favourite chutneys, if desired.

MIRCHI VADA

Deep-fried green chillies stuffed with spicy potato mash

• Ingredients •

- → 1 cup (225 g) potatoes, mashed
- → 1 medium-size green chilli, finely chopped
- → 1 Tbsp (6 g) ground coriander (*dhaniya*)
- → 2 tsp red chilli powder
- → 2 tsp dried mango powder (*amchoor*)
- → 2 tsp fennel (*saunf*) seeds
- → 1 tsp chaat masala

- → 1 tsp ground cumin (*jeera*)
- → Salt, to taste
- → 10 large green chillies, slit, seeded
- → 1 cup (120 g) chickpea flour (*besan*)
- → Water, as needed
- → Vegetable oil, for deep-frying

• Method •

1 In a medium-size bowl, stir together the mashed potatoes, chopped green chilli, coriander, red chilli powder, dried mango powder, fennel seeds, chaat masala, and cumin. Season to taste with salt. Stuff the large chillies with this mixture.

2 In a small bowl, mix the chickpea flour, salt, and enough water to make a pancake-like batter.

3 In a deep skillet over medium-high heat, heat the vegetable oil for deep-frying. Working in batches, dip the stuffed chillies into the batter and carefully add them to the hot oil. Deep-fry until golden. Transfer to paper towels to drain. Serve hot, with your favourite chutneys, if desired.

COCONUT CHUTNEY

An indispensable accompaniment to food in South Indian cuisine, always made with fresh coconut

• Ingredients •

- → 1 cup (80 g) fresh coconut, grated

- → 2 green chillies, finely chopped

- → 1 tsp ginger paste

- → Salt, to taste

- → 1 Tbsp (15 ml) coconut oil

- → 1 Tbsp (13 g) Bengal gram (*chana dal*), roasted

- → 1 tsp mustard (*rai*) seeds

- → 1 dried red chilli (*sookhi lal mirch*)

- → 3 curry leaves (*kadhi patta*)

• Method •

1 In a food processor, blend the coconut, green chillies, ginger, and salt. Add a little water to adjust consistency. It should resemble a thick porridge and be coarse.

2 In a skillet over medium-high heat, heat the coconut oil. Add the Bengal gram, mustard seeds, dried red chilli, and curry leaves, and allow the ingredients to crackle.

3 Pour this hot tempering on the coconut mixture and stir well.

MUMBAI VEGETABLE SANDWICH

Popular and wholesome Mumbai street food

• Ingredients •

- → 1 medium-size beetroot

- → 1 medium-size cucumber

- → 2 medium-size potatoes, boiled, thinly sliced

- → 1 medium-size tomato

- → 4 slices brown bread

- → Butter (at room temperature), to taste

- → 1 Tbsp (15 g) green chutney (available at grocery stores)

- → Black salt (*kala namak*), to taste

- → Pinch roasted cumin (*jeera*) powder, optional

- → Ground black pepper (*kali mirch*), to taste, optional

- → Ketchup, to taste, optional

• Method •

1 In a saucepan over medium heat, heat water. Peel the beetroot and cook in water until soft but crisp.

2 Thinly slice the cucumber, tomato and beetroot.

3 Butter both sides of the bread slices evenly. Spread one side with a generous amount of green chutney and then pile a few slices of cucumber, beetroot, potatoes and tomato.

4 Sprinkle with black salt, roasted cumin powder and pepper and cover with another slice of bread. Serve with green chutney and ketchup, if desired.

BREAD PAKORA
Bread fritters

• Ingredients •

- → 4-5 bread slices
- → 1 cup (120 g) chickpea flour (*besan*)
- → ¼ tsp turmeric (*haldi*) powder
- → Salt, to taste
- → ½ tsp carom (*ajwain*) seeds

- → Red chilli powder, to taste
- → ¼ tsp garam masala
- → Water
- → Vegetable oil, for frying

• Method •

1 Cut the bread slices into desired shapes (like triangle, rectangle, etc.).

2 In a bowl, mix the chickpea flour, turmeric powder, salt, carom seeds, red chilli powder, and garam masala.

3 Add a little water to make a smooth batter of coating consistency.

4 In a wok over medium heat, heat the oil for frying.

5 Dip the bread slices in the batter and carefully slip one slice at a time in the hot oil.

6 Deep-fry until crisp and golden brown.

7 Remove and drain on paper towels. Serve hot with your favourite chutneys and tomato ketchup, if desired.

BEDMI PURI
Fried and crispy breakfast bread

· Ingredients ·

- → 1½ cups plus 2 Tbsp (200 g) whole-wheat flour (*atta*)

- → ½ cup (100 g) split black gram (*dhuli urad dal*), soaked in water for 3 hours, drained, and ground to a coarse paste

- → 1 Tbsp (15 ml) vegetable oil, plus more for frying

- → 2 Tbsp (22 g) semolina (*suji*)

- → 1 Tbsp (10 g) rice flour

- → 1 tsp ground fennel (*saunf*) seeds

- → 1 tsp red chilli powder

- → 1 tsp ground coriander (*dhaniya*)

- → ¼ cup (4 g) green coriander (*hara dhaniya*) leaves, finely chopped

- → Water, as needed

· Method ·

1 In a medium-size bowl, combine the wheat flour, split black gram paste, vegetable oil, semolina, rice flour, ground fennel seeds, red chilli powder, ground coriander, and coriander leaves. Mix well.

2 Add enough water to knead the mixture into a tight dough. Divide the dough into 8 small balls and roll them into small puris.

3 In a deep skillet over medium-high heat, heat the vegetable oil for frying.

4 Carefully add the puris to the hot oil and fry until golden on both sides. Serve hot with your favourite potato dish, if desired.

ALOO KI SUBJI

*A no-fuss potato curry served with deep-fried breads —
a best-seller in all railway stations*

• Ingredients •

→ 4½ cups (500 g) potatoes, boiled, peeled, diced

→ 1 Tbsp (15 ml) vegetable oil

→ 1 tsp cumin (*jeera*) seeds

→ 2 tsp turmeric (*haldi*) powder

→ 2 tsp red chilli powder

→ Salt, to taste

→ 3 cups (720 ml) hot water

• Method •

1 In a wok over medium heat, heat the vegetable oil.

2 Add the cumin seeds, potatoes, turmeric powder, red chilli powder, salt and hot water. Mix well and cook for 15 minutes on medium heat or till the gravy is semi-thick.

3 Serve hot with bedmi puri (p. 25).

CHAAT PAPDI
Flour crispies topped with yoghurt

• Ingredients •

→ 1 cup (125 g) refined flour (*maida*)

→ 1 Tbsp (11 g) semolina (*suji*)

→ Salt, to taste

→ Pinch baking powder

→ ¾ cup (180 ml) vegetable oil

→ Water, for kneading

→ Vegetable oil, for frying

→ ½ cup (55 g) potatoes, boiled, cubed

→ ½ cup (100 g) chickpeas (*kabuli chana*), boiled

→ ¾ cup (150 g) tamarind (*imli*) chutney (available at grocery stores)

→ 4 Tbsp (60 g) mint (*pudina*) chutney (p. 50)

→ 1 cup (240 g) yoghurt (*dahi*), beaten

→ Chaat masala, to taste

• Method •

1 In a large bowl, sift the refined flour, semolina, salt, and baking powder together.

2 Warm ¾ cup of vegetable oil and add it to the flour mixture. Knead with enough water to make a smooth dough.

3 Divide the dough equally into tiny balls. Roll each out into very thin discs of 1½ in. diameter. Perforate each with a fork so that they do not puff out while frying. Set aside for 30 minutes, uncovered.

4 In a wok over medium heat, heat the vegetable oil for deep-frying. Carefully slip the discs in one at a time into the hot oil. Deep-fry the discs until crisp and golden. Remove with a slotted spoon and drain on paper towels.

5 To serve, arrange the fried discs (papdi) on a plate; place the potatoes and chickpeas on top. Drizzle the tamarind and mint chutneys and yoghurt. Finally, sprinkle chaat masala.

SHAKARKANDI KI CHAAT

Tangy sweet potatoes

• Ingredients •

- → 4½ cups (500 g) sweet potatoes, boiled, cubed

- → 2 tsp salt

- → ½ cup (100 g) tomatoes, chopped

- → 2 Tbsp (30 ml) lemon juice

- → 4 green chillies, chopped

- → ½ cup (8 g) green coriander (*hara dhaniya*), chopped

- → 1 small bunch mint (*pudina*) leaves, chopped

- → 2 tsp dried mango powder (*amchoor*)

• Method •

1 In a large bowl, mix salt, tomatoes, lemon juice, green chillies, green coriander, and mint leaves.

2 Add sweet potatoes and mix well.

3 Sprinkle mango powder over the mixture and serve.

ALOO PARATHA
Potato-stuffed unleavened bread

• Ingredients •

- → 1 medium-size onion, finely chopped

- → 1 medium-size green chilli, finely chopped

- → 1 cup (225 g) potatoes, boiled and mashed well

- → 1 tsp ground coriander (*dhaniya*)

- → 1 tsp dried mango powder (*amchoor*)

- → Salt, to taste

- → 1 cup (125 g) whole-wheat flour (*atta*)

- → 2 Tbsp (30 g) ghee

• Method •

1 In a medium-size bowl, combine the onion, green chilli, potatoes, coriander, and dried mango powder. Season to taste with salt.

2 In another medium-size bowl, knead the flour with just enough water to form a soft dough.

3 Divide the dough into equal portions and roll out each small ball of dough into a small disc. Place the potato filling in the centre.

4 Bring the edges together and pat it flat with your palm. Roll once again into a larger paratha.

5 Heat a griddle over high heat until very hot.

6 Heat the ghee and pan-fry the paratha on both sides until golden.

7 Serve with pickle, yoghurt and butter, if desired.

PHAL KI CHAAT

Mixed fruit delight

• Ingredients •

- → 2 apples, cored, diced
- → 2 pears, cored, diced
- → 1 medium-size banana, peeled, thickly cut
- → ½ medium-size papaya, peeled, deseeded, diced
- → 1 medium-size mango, peeled, diced
- → 1 large potato, boiled, peeled, diced

- → 1 medium-size cucumber, peeled, diced
- → 1 tsp lemon juice
- → 2 tsp black salt
- → ½ tsp red chilli powder
- → 1 tsp tamarind (*imli*) pulp
- → 1 tsp chaat masala
- → Few mint (*pudina*) leaves for garnishing

• Method •

1 In a large bowl, mix all the chopped fruits and vegetables together.

2 Add lemon juice, black salt, and red chilli powder. Mix and set aside for 10 minutes.

3 Serve with a dressing of tamarind pulp. Sprinkle chaat masala and garnish with mint leaves.

CHEF'S NOTE

1 tsp lightly roasted and powdered cumin seeds may also be added. This preparation must be made fresh, almost before being served, to retain the crispness of the fruits. Any combination of seasonal fruits may be used.

MASALA UTTAPAM
Spicy rice and black gram pancakes

• Ingredients •

For the batter:

→ ¾ cup (150 g) rice (soaked in water for at least 5 hours)

→ ¾ cup (150 g) split black gram (*dhuli urad dal*), soaked in water for at least 3 hours

→ Salt, to taste

For the filling:

→ ¼ cup (60 ml) vegetable oil

→ 1 large onion, finely chopped

→ 2 large tomatoes, finely chopped

→ 4 green chillies, finely chopped

→ 1 tsp cumin (*jeera*) seeds

→ 2 Tbsp (2 g) green coriander (*hara dhaniya*), finely chopped

→ Salt, to taste

• Method •

1 For the batter: In a food processor, grind together the rice, split black gram, salt and a little water. Make into a batter and set aside. Cover and ferment for 8–12 hours.

2 For the filling: In a medium-size skillet over medium heat, heat a little oil. Add onion, tomatoes, green chillies, cumin seeds, green coriander, and salt to taste. Mix thoroughly and cook for a few minutes. Keep the filling aside.

3 In a non-stick skillet over medium heat, heat enough vegetable oil for pan-frying.

4 Pour a ladleful of the batter and spread it evenly. Cook on medium heat. Spread the filling on the batter, sprinkle a little oil around the sides and cook until the pancake is brown on the underside. Turn and cook the other side as well. Repeat till all the batter is used up. Serve hot with *sambhar* and your favourite chutneys.

CHEF'S NOTE

You can buy ready-made batter from a grocery store as well.

ALOO TIKKI

Spiced potato patties

• Ingredients •

- → 2 potatoes, boiled, mashed
- → 2 tsp red chilli powder
- → 2 tsp ground coriander (*dhaniya*)
- → 2 tsp chaat masala

- → 2 tsp ground cumin (*jeera*)
- → 1 tsp black salt (*kala namak*)
- → Salt, to taste
- → Vegetable oil, for frying

• Method •

1 In a medium-size bowl, stir together the potatoes, red chilli powder, coriander, chaat masala, cumin, black salt, and salt.

2 Divide the mixture into equal lemon-size portions. Grease your palms and roll each portion to make a ball, then flatten into a smooth, round patty about ½ in. thick.

3 In a skillet over medium-high heat, heat the oil. Working in batches, add the patties to the hot skillet and pan-fry on both sides until golden brown.

4 Serve hot with mint chutney (p. 50), if desired.

KASURI PANEER TIKKA
Cottage cheese cubes flavoured with fenugreek

• Ingredients •

- 2 lb, 3 oz (1 kg) cottage cheese (*paneer*)
- 1 tsp black cumin (*shah jeera*) seeds
- 1 tsp white pepper (*safed mirch*) powder
- 2 tsp garam masala
- 5 tsp lemon juice
- Salt, to taste
- ¼ cup (60 g) cottage cheese (*paneer*), grated
- ½ cup (120 ml) cream

- ¾ cup (180 g) yoghurt (*dahi*), hung
- 2 Tbsp (15 g) chickpea flour (*besan*) or cornflour
- 4 tsp dried fenugreek leaves (*kasuri methi*)
- 2 tsp chaat masala, optional
- 2 Tbsp (30 g) ginger-garlic (*adrak-lasan*) paste
- 2 tsp red chilli powder
- Butter, to baste

• Method •

1 Wash and cut the cottage cheese into 1.5 in. cubes.

2 Mix black cumin seeds, white pepper, garam masala, 4 tsp lemon juice, and salt together. Mix in grated cottage cheese and refrigerate for 1 hour.

3 Whisk the remaining ingredients (except butter) to a fine batter. Add the cottage cheese cubes, mix well and marinade for at least 1 hour.

4 Preheat the oven to 150°C (300°F). Put the cubes 1 in. apart on a skewer. Roast in an oven, tandoor or charcoal grill for 5–6 minutes. Baste with butter.

5 Serve hot, sprinkled with chaat masala and remaining lemon juice, accompanied with mint chutney (p. 50).

KHANDVI

Bite-size chickpea and yoghurt rolls tempered with sesame seeds

• Ingredients •

- → 1 Tbsp (15 ml) vegetable oil, plus more for greasing the plate
- → 1 cup (120 g) chickpea flour (*besan*)
- → ¼ cup (60 g) yoghurt (*dahi*)
- → 1 tsp ground turmeric (*haldi*)
- → 1 tsp red chilli powder
- → Pinch ground asafoetida (*hing*)

- → 3 cups (720 ml) water
- → Salt, to taste
- → 1 tsp mustard (*rai*) seeds
- → 1 tsp white sesame (*safed til*) seeds
- → 1 medium-size green chilli, finely chopped
- → ¼ cup (4 g) green coriander (*hara dhaniya*) leaves, finely chopped

• Method •

1 Grease a rimmed plate with some vegetable oil and set aside.

2 In a bowl, stir together the chickpea flour, yoghurt, turmeric, red chilli powder, asafoetida, water, and salt, stirring continuously until you have a lump-free mixture.

3 Place a saucepan over medium heat and pour in the flour mixture. Cook, stirring continuously, until the mixture thickens. Pour a thin layer onto the prepared plate. Set aside for 10 minutes to cool, or until it hardens but is still warm. With a sharp knife,

cut the hardened mixture into about 10 strips. Roll each strip like a roulade. Repeat with the remaining flour mixture, cooling, cutting, and rolling.

4 In a skillet over low-medium heat, heat the vegetable oil.

5 Add the mustard seeds, white sesame seeds, and green chilli. Cook until the seeds begin to crackle. Pour the tempering over the rolled strips (khandvi). Serve warm or cold, garnished with fresh coriander.

BHUTTA

Roasted corn on cob — there is nothing to match this simple pleasure in life

• Ingredients •

→ 6 ears of corn, fresh, tender, peeled

→ Butter, optional

→ 3 tsp salt

→ 2 tsp red chilli powder

→ 1 lemon, halved

• Method •

1 Place the corn directly on the fire on a hob. Keep rotating it so that it cooks evenly. Remove when brown.

2 Smear with butter, salt and red chilli powder, and rub the lemon over it.

3 Serve warm.

CHEF'S NOTE

The best result is obtained by cooking the corn on embers of charcoal fire or the barbecue.

POHA

Street-style spiced flattened rice

• Ingredients •

- → 1 Tbsp (15 ml) vegetable oil
- → 1 tsp mustard (*rai*) seeds
- → 1 tsp cumin (*jeera*) seeds
- → 1 tsp fennel (*saunf*) seeds
- → 2 curry leaves (*kadhi patta*)
- → 1 medium-size green chilli, finely chopped
- → 1 tsp ground turmeric (*haldi*)

- → 1 tsp red chilli powder
- → 1 tsp fresh ginger, grated, peeled
- → 1 tsp garlic, grated
- → ½ cup (88 g) onions, finely chopped
- → 2 cups (400 g) flattened rice (*poha* or *chura*)
- → Salt, to taste
- → ¼ cup (4 g) green coriander (*hara dhaniya*) leaves, finely chopped

• Method •

1 In a skillet over low-medium heat, heat the vegetable oil.

2 Add the mustard seeds, cumin seeds, fennel seeds, curry leaves, and green chilli. Cook until the seeds begin to crackle.

3 Stir in the turmeric, red chilli powder, ginger, garlic, and onions. Sauté until fragrant.

4 Add the flattened rice. Stir until everything turns a sunny yellow. Cook for 2–3 minutes.

5 Season to taste with salt and garnish with green coriander before serving.

UPMA

Semolina tempered with mustard seeds

• Ingredients •

- → 2 cups (340 g) semolina (*suji*)

- → ¼ cup (60 ml) vegetable oil

- → ½ tsp mustard (*rai*) seeds

- → 1 dried red chilli (*sookhi lal mirch*)

- → 1½ tsp black gram (*urad dal*)

- → 3 Tbsp (30 g) onions, finely chopped

- → 2 green chillies, chopped into rounds

- → 1 tsp ginger, finely chopped

- → Few curry leaves (*kadhi patta*)

- → 4 cups (960 ml) water

- → Salt, to taste

• Method •

1 In a skillet over low-medium heat, heat 1 Tbsp of vegetable oil. Roast the semolina on low heat for some time (it should not change colour).

2 In a separate pan, heat the remaining oil. Add mustard seeds, dried red chilli, black gram, onions, green chillies, ginger, and curry leaves. Sauté for 3-4 minutes.

3 Pour in the water. Add salt and bring the mixture to a boil. Now add the roasted semolina.

4 Lower heat and keep stirring continuously so that the mixture is lump-free. Cook till all the water has been absorbed and the mixture is absolutely dry. Serve hot.

MOONG BHAJIYA

Spiced lentil fritters

• Ingredients •

→ 1 cup (200 g) split yellow gram (*moong dhuli*), soaked in water overnight, drained

→ 1 cup (225 g) potatoes, mashed

→ 2 green chillies, finely chopped

→ 1 Tbsp (15 g) ginger-garlic (*adrak-lasan*) paste

→ ¼ cup (4 g) green coriander (*hara dhaniya*) leaves, finely chopped

→ ¼ cup (43 g) onions, finely chopped

→ Salt, to taste

→ Freshly ground black pepper (*kali mirch*), to taste

→ Vegetable oil, for frying

• Method •

1 In a food processor, combine the split yellow gram, potatoes, green chillies, and ginger-garlic paste. Blend for a few seconds until you get a slightly chunky consistency. Transfer the mixture to a medium-size bowl.

2 Stir in the coriander and onions. Season to taste with salt and pepper.

3 In a deep skillet over medium heat, heat the vegetable oil for frying.

4 Carefully drop spoonfuls of the prepared mixture into the hot oil (should make 10 small fritters). Gently fry until beautifully golden. Transfer to paper towels to drain. Serve hot with your favourite chutneys, if desired.

BONDA
Typical spicy snack

• Ingredients •

- → 2 cups (450 g) potatoes, boiled, mashed
- → 6 green chillies, chopped
- → 1 Tbsp (1 g) green coriander (*hara dhaniya*) leaves, finely chopped
- → 1 Tbsp (15 g) yoghurt (*dahi*)
- → 1 tsp fresh ginger, chopped, peeled
- → Pinch ground asafoetida (*hing*)
- → Salt, to taste

- → 1 cup (125 g) refined flour (*maida*)
- → ½ cup (60 g) chickpea flour (*besan*)
- → ½ cup (80 g) rice flour
- → Pinch baking soda
- → Water, as needed
- → Vegetable oil, for frying

• Method •

1 In a medium-size bowl, stir together the mashed potatoes, green chillies, green coriander, yoghurt, ginger, and asafoetida. Season to taste with salt. Shape the mixture into medium-size balls.

2 In another medium-size bowl, stir together the flours, baking soda, and enough water to make a semi-thick batter.

3 In a wok over medium heat, heat the vegetable oil for frying.

4 Working in small batches, dip the potato balls into the batter and then carefully lower them into the hot oil.

5 Cook until crisp. With a slotted spoon, transfer to paper towels to drain.

6 Serve hot with your favourite chutneys.

DHUSKA

Deep-fried rice and dal dumplings

• Ingredients •

- → 2 cups (400 g) basmati rice

- → 1 cup (200 g) split Bengal gram (*chana dal*), soaked in water for 2 hours, drained

- → 2 green chillies, finely chopped

- → 1 Tbsp (15 g) garlic, finely chopped

- → ½ cup (120 ml) water

- → 1 tsp ground turmeric (*haldi*)

- → 4 curry leaves (*kadhi patta*)

- → ¼ cup (4 g) green coriander (*hara dhaniya*) leaves, finely chopped

- → 1 medium-size onion, finely chopped

- → Salt, to taste

- → Vegetable oil, for frying

• Method •

1 In a food processor, combine the rice, split Bengal gram, green chillies, garlic, and water. Blend into a thick paste.

2 Add the turmeric, curry leaves, green coriander, and onion. Season to taste with salt. Blend to combine. Separate the paste into 10–15 balls.

3 In a skillet over medium heat, heat the vegetable oil. Add the balls and fry until golden brown.

4 Serve hot with any gravy dish or your favourite chutneys or pickle, if desired.

FRIED GARADU

Indore-style spiced yam wedges

• Ingredients •

→ Vegetable oil, for frying

→ 2 cups (220 g) yam, cubed

→ 1 Tbsp (10 g) *jiralu* masala (available at grocery stores)

→ Juice of 1 lemon

→ Salt, to taste

→ ¼ cup (4 g) green coriander (*hara dhaniya*) leaves, finely chopped

• Method •

1 In a skillet over low-medium heat, heat the vegetable oil for frying.

2 Carefully add the yams to the hot oil and deep-fry until golden brown. Transfer to paper towels to drain and sprinkle with the *jiralu* masala, lemon juice, and salt.

3 Garnish with green coriander and serve hot.

BESAN KA CHILA

Chickpea pancakes with cottage cheese

• Ingredients •

- → ½ cup (60 g) chickpea flour (*besan*)
- → 1 medium-size onion, chopped
- → 1 medium-size tomato, chopped
- → 1 medium-size green chilli, finely chopped
- → 1 tsp red chilli powder
- → 1 tsp chaat masala
- → 1 tsp ground cumin (*jeera*)

- → 1 tsp turmeric (*haldi*)
- → Salt, to taste
- → ¼ cup (4 g) green coriander (*hara dhaniya*) leaves, finely chopped
- → Water, as needed
- → ½ cup (113 g) cottage cheese (*paneer*)
- → 1 Tbsp (15 ml) vegetable oil

• Method •

1 In a medium-size bowl, combine the chickpea flour, green chilli, cumin, turmeric, red chilli powder and coriander leaves.

2 Season to taste with salt. Stir in enough water to achieve a pancake-batter-like consistency.

3 Cut the paneer into small cubes and mix with tomato and onion.

4 In a skillet over medium heat, heat the vegetable oil.

5 Pour in the batter and spread to make a pancake of 7 in. diameter. Cook on both sides until golden brown. Sprinkle a little oil to prevent the pancake from sticking to the pan.

6 Sprinkle some of the cottage cheese mixture on top and remove from the heat.

7 Repeat the same process with the rest of the batter and cottage cheese mixture. Serve hot.

METHI THEPLA

Thin chapatti flavoured with fenugreek

• Ingredients •

→ 1 cup (125 g) whole-wheat flour (*atta*)

→ ¼ cup (15 g) fresh fenugreek (*methi*) leaves, finely chopped

→ 2 Tbsp (30 g) yoghurt (*dahi*)

→ 1 Tbsp (15 ml) vegetable oil

→ 2 tsp ginger-chilli (*adrak-mirch*) paste

→ 1 tsp red chilli powder

→ 1 tsp ground turmeric (*haldi*)

→ 1 tsp white sesame (*safed til*) seeds

→ Salt, to taste

→ Water, for kneading

• Method •

1 In a medium-size bowl, mix the whole-wheat flour, fenugreek leaves, yoghurt, vegetable oil, ginger-chilli paste, red chilli powder, turmeric, white sesame seeds, salt, and enough water to knead the mixture into a soft dough. Divide the dough into 6 balls and roll each into a thin disc about the size of your palm.

2 Heat a griddle over medium heat until hot.

3 Place the discs on the griddle and cook for 3–4 minutes on both sides. Serve hot or cold.

ALOO KABLI

Potato and chickpea delight — a popular Kolkata snack

• Ingredients •

→ 2¾ cups (300 g) potatoes, boiled, peeled, diced

→ 1 cup (200 g) chickpeas (*kabuli chana*), soaked in water overnight

→ 1 tsp dried mango powder (*amchoor*)

→ 1 tsp cumin (*jeera*) powder

→ 2 tsp coriander (*dhaniya*) powder

→ 1 tsp rock salt (*kala namak*)

→ ½ tsp red chilli powder

→ ½ tsp lemon juice

→ Salt, to taste

For the garnish:

→ 1 Tbsp (24 g) ginger, julienned

→ 1 Tbsp (15 g) green chillies, finely sliced

→ Lemon, cut into wedges

• Method •

1 Drain the chickpeas and pressure cook with 2 cups of water for about 10 minutes or till soft. Drain and set aside.

2 Mix all the ingredients thoroughly in a bowl.

3 Serve cold, garnished with ginger, green chillies and lemon wedges.

CHURA MATTAR

Flattened rice soaked in milk and cream, tempered, and tossed with green peas

• Ingredients •

→ ½ cup (120 ml) milk

→ ½ cup (120 ml) heavy cream

→ 1 cup (200 g) flattened rice (*poha* or *chura*), rinsed

→ 1 Tbsp (15 g) ghee

→ 1 tsp cumin (*jeera*) seeds

→ 1 tsp ginger paste

→ 1 medium-size green chilli, finely chopped

→ ½ cup (80 g) green peas, boiled

→ 1 tsp garam masala

→ 1 tsp chaat masala

→ 1 tsp freshly ground black pepper (*kali mirch*)

→ Salt, to taste

→ Juice of 1 lemon

• Method •

1 In a medium-size bowl, combine the milk and cream. Add the rice and soak for 8 minutes. Drain. Save the milk and cream mixture to add to rich curries later, if desired.

2 In a skillet over medium-high heat, heat the ghee.

3 Add the cumin seeds. Cook until the seeds begin to crackle.

4 Add the ginger paste and green chilli. Stir-fry for 1 minute.

5 Add the boiled green peas. Cook for 5–7 minutes.

6 Stir in the garam masala, chaat masala, and pepper. Season to taste with salt. Add the soaked rice. Cook for 3–4 minutes until the rice is soft. Mix in the lemon juice and serve.

PAO BHAJI

Mashed potatoes served with bread rolls

• Ingredients •

- → 2 lb, 3 oz (1 kg) potatoes, boiled, peeled, diced

- → 1 cup (240 g or 240 ml) ghee or vegetable oil

- → 2 cups (480 g) tomatoes, washed, diced

- → ½ cup (85 g) onions, finely chopped

- → 6 green chillies, chopped, with or without seeds

- → 1½ Tbsp (23 g) ginger, peeled, minced

- → 1½ tsp turmeric (*haldi*) powder

- → 1 tsp red chilli powder

- → Salt, to taste

- → 2 tsp garlic paste

- → 2 tsp ginger paste

- → 1 cup (240 ml) water

- → ¾ cup (100 g) butter

- → 2 tsp garam masala

- → 1 cup (16 g) green coriander (*hara dhaniya*), chopped

- → 3 Tbsp (45 ml) lemon juice

- → 12 bread rolls (*pao*), cut horizontally

- → Water, as needed

• Method •

1 In a large skillet over medium heat, heat the ghee or oil.

2 Add the tomatoes, onions, green chillies, ginger, and turmeric powder. Stir-fry for 4-5 minutes on medium heat.

3 Dilute the ginger and garlic pastes, each in ½ cup of water.

4 Add the potatoes, red chilli powder, and salt. Mix thoroughly and continue to cook on low heat, mashing and stirring for 6-7 minutes with a spatula. Add the garlic and ginger pastes diluted in water. Increase heat and add 4 Tbsp of butter. Mix well.

5 Lastly, add the garam masala, green coriander, and lemon juice. Stir well.

6 Before serving, coat the bread roll halves with the remaining butter and fry them face down on the griddle or frying pan until they are lightly browned. Serve these bread rolls with the bhaji (potato mixture).

AMRITSARI KULCHA

Flatbread stuffed with potato and paneer

• Ingredients •

For the dough:

→ 1 cup (125 g) refined flour (*maida*)

→ 1 tsp sugar

→ 1 tsp baking powder

→ ½ tsp baking soda

→ 3 Tbsp (45 g) ghee

→ ¼ cup (60 g) yoghurt (*dahi*)

→ ¼ cup (60 ml) milk

→ Salt, to taste

For the filling:

→ 1 cup (225 g) potatoes, mashed

→ 1 medium-size green chilli, finely chopped

→ 1 tsp ground cumin (*jeera*)

→ 1 tsp red chilli powder

→ 1 tsp chaat masala

→ ½ medium-size onion, finely chopped

→ ¼ cup (4 g) green coriander (*hara dhaniya*) leaves, finely chopped

→ ¼ cup (60 g) cottage cheese (*paneer*), finely chopped

→ Salt, to taste

→ Butter, for serving

• *Method* •

1 For the dough: In a medium-size bowl, combine the flour, sugar, baking powder, baking soda, ghee, yoghurt, and milk. Season to taste with salt. Mix together and knead into a medium-soft dough. Set aside for 1 hour.

2 For the filling: In another medium-size bowl, stir together the mashed potatoes, green chilli, cumin, red chilli powder, chaat masala, onion, coriander leaves, and cottage cheese. Season to taste with salt.

3 Divide the dough into 4 small balls. Roll each into a 4 in. disc. Place a spoonful of filling in the centre of each and join all the edges to seal the filling inside.

4 Roll it back into a ball, the size of your palm, and pat it with your fingertips.

5 Heat a griddle over medium-high heat.

6 Working in batches, cook the stuffed discs on both sides until golden brown. Serve hot, with lots of butter.

BHELPURI

Tangy puffed rice mixture

• Ingredients •

→ 1 cup (240 g) puffed rice (*murmura*, available at grocery stores)

→ ½ cup (60 g) chickpea flour (*besan*) or chickpea vermicelli (available at grocery stores)

→ 2 medium-size potatoes, boiled, peeled, diced

→ 1 medium-size onion, chopped

→ Tamarind (*imli*) chutney (available at grocery stores)

→ ½ cup (120 ml) water, cold

For the flat pastries (papdi):

→ ½ cup (63 g) whole-wheat flour (*atta*)

→ ½ cup (85 g) semolina (*suji*)

→ 1 tsp onion seeds (*kalonji*), powdered

→ Salt, to taste

→ 1 tsp vegetable oil

→ ½ cup (120 ml) water, cold

For the mint chutney:

→ 2 cups (250 g) mint (*pudina*) leaves, no stems

→ 1 medium-size onion, peeled, chopped

→ 3 green chillies, chopped

→ 1 Tbsp (15 ml) lemon juice

→ Salt, to taste

→ 2 tsp sugar, optional

• Method •

1 In a large bowl, mix the puffed rice and chickpea flour or chickpea vermicelli together. Set aside.

2 For the flat pastries (papdi): In a large bowl, mix the whole-wheat flour, semolina, onion seed powder and salt. Knead with water to form a medium-soft dough. Divide the dough equally into marble-size balls. Using a rolling pin, roll out into thin round discs without coating with flour. Prick the discs all over with a fork.

3 In a wok over low-medium heat, heat the oil. Deep-fry the discs, a few at a time. When golden and crisp on both sides, remove with a slotted spoon. Drain on paper towels. Repeat until all are done.

4 For the mint chutney: With a pestle and mortar or food processor, grind or blend all the ingredients together with water to make a thick, smooth paste. Set aside.

5 To assemble the bhelpuri: Add the fried pastries, potatoes and onion to the puffed rice mixture. Add the mint chutney and tamarind chutney, mix well and serve immediately.

SPICY DAHI VADAS, SOUTH INDIAN STYLE

Famous savoury snack

· Ingredients ·

For the dumplings (vadas):

→ 2 cups (400 g) split black gram (*dhuli urad dal*), soaked in water overnight, drained

→ Salt, to taste

→ ½ cup (32 g) curry leaves (*kadhi patta*), chopped

→ 2 green chillies, finely chopped

→ 1 Tbsp (15 g) crushed, peeled fresh ginger

→ 1 Tbsp (15 ml) freshly squeezed lemon juice

→ ½ tsp ground asafoetida (*hing*) stirred into ½ cup (120 ml) water

For the spice mix:

→ 2 dried red chillies (*sookhi lal mirch*)

→ 1 tsp cumin (*jeera*) seeds

→ ½ tsp black mustard (*rai*) seeds

For the yoghurt (dahi):

→ 2 tsp vegetable oil

→ ½ cup (32 g) curry leaves (*kadhi patta*), chopped

→ 4 green chillies

→ 3 cups (720 g) yoghurt (*dahi*)

→ 1 cup (240 ml) water

→ Salt, to taste

→ Vegetable oil, for deep-frying

• Method •

1 For the dumplings (vadas): In a blender or food processor, grind the split black gram to a paste. Add salt, the curry leaves, green chillies, ginger, lemon juice, and asafoetida water. Blend into a stiff batter and set aside.

2 For the spice mix: In a blender or with a mortar and pestle, coarsely crush the dried red chillies, cumin seeds, and mustard seeds.

3 For the yoghurt (dahi): In a wok over low-medium heat, heat the vegetable oil.

4 Add the coarsely crushed spice mix, curry leaves, and green chillies. Cook for a few seconds.

5 Stir in the yoghurt and water. Season to taste with salt. Transfer to a bowl and set aside.

6 Clean the wok and return it to the heat. Heat the vegetable oil for deep-frying.

7 Have a bowl of cold water nearby. Gently lower spoonfuls of the black gram batter into the hot oil and deep-fry the vadas until golden. Remove and drain on paper towels. Transfer the vadas to the water for just a few seconds. Remove and gently squeeze out the excess water. Repeat with the remaining batter.

8 Add the vadas to the spiced yoghurt and serve cold.

LITTI CHOKHA

Rustic dish of sattu-stuffed whole-wheat balls

• Ingredients •

For the tomato and potato vegetable mix (chokha):

→ 1 medium-size tomato, finely chopped

→ 1 cup (225 g) potatoes, mashed coarsely

→ Juice of 1 lemon

→ 2 Tbsp (2 g) green coriander (*hara dhaniya*) leaves, finely chopped

→ 1 Tbsp (15 ml) mustard (*rai*) oil

→ 1 tsp freshly ground black pepper (*kali mirch*)

→ 1 tsp ginger paste

→ 1 medium-size green chilli, finely chopped

→ Salt, to taste

For the filling:

→ ¾ cup (95 g) *sattu* (available at grocery stores)

→ ½ cup (120 ml) water

→ 1 Tbsp (15 g) ghee

→ 1 tsp ground turmeric (*haldi*)

→ 1 tsp red chilli powder

→ 1 tsp dried mango powder (*amchoor*)

→ 1 tsp fresh ginger, grated, peeled

→ 1 tsp green chilli, finely chopped

→ Pinch ground asafoetida (*hing*)

For the dough (litti):

→ 1 cup (125 g) whole-wheat flour (*atta*)

→ 3 Tbsp (45 g) ghee, plus more for serving

→ Salt, to taste

→ Water, for kneading

· Method ·

1 Preheat the oven to 150°C (300°F).

2 For the tomato and potato vegetable mix (chokha): Using two small bowls, put the tomato in one bowl and the potatoes in the other. Divide each of the remaining chokha ingredients evenly between the two bowls. Season each to taste with salt. Stir each bowl to combine its ingredients. Your tomato and potato chokha are ready. Set aside.

3 For the filling: In a medium-size bowl, stir together all the ingredients. Set aside.

4 For the dough (litti): In a small bowl, stir together all the ingredients with enough water to form a smooth dough. Separate the dough into 6 table-tennis-ball-size balls.

5 Flatten the dough balls with your finger.

6 Place a spoonful of the filling in the centre of each ball. Roll the balls back into shape and place on a baking sheet. Bake for 30 minutes at 150°C (300°F).

7 Serve the litti with the chokha and lots of ghee.

MASALA DOSA

Stuffed Savoury Pancakes

· Ingredients ·

For the batter:

→ ¾ cup (150 g) rice, soaked in water overnight, parboiled

→ ¾ cup (150 g) black gram (*urad dal*), soaked in water overnight

→ 1 tsp fenugreek seeds (*methi dana*)

→ Salt, to taste

For the filling:

→ 1¾ cups (400 g) potatoes, boiled, peeled and roughly mashed using hands

→ 2 Tbsp (30 ml) vegetable oil

→ 1 tsp black mustard (*rai*) seeds

→ ½ tsp fenugreek seeds (*methi dana*)

→ ¾ cup (125 g) onions, finely sliced

→ 2 tsp turmeric (*haldi*) powder

→ ½ tsp red chilli powder

→ 2 green chillies, finely chopped, optional

→ Ghee or vegetable oil, for frying

• Method •

1 For the batter: Drain the rice. In a food processor, blend it to a semi-thick paste (the paste should feel a bit grainy).

2 Drain the black gram. In a food processor, blend it with the fenugreek seeds to a fine paste.

3 Mix the rice paste and black gram–fenugreek paste together. Add salt. Let the mixture stand overnight.

4 For the filling: Heat the vegetable oil in a wok.

5 Add the mustard and fenugreek seeds. When they start crackling, add the onions. Sauté for a few minutes until the onions turn translucent.

6 Add the turmeric powder, mashed potatoes, red chilli powder and green chillies (if using). Fry for a minute. Set aside.

7 In a non-stick frying pan over low-medium heat, add the vegetable oil or ghee for pan-frying.

8 Pour a ladleful or rounded spoonful of the batter in the centre. Spread the batter in a circular motion with the back of the spoon to cover the surface. Cook on medium heat until the underside is golden, spreading some ghee or oil in the centre and along the sides.

9 Place 2 Tbsp of the potato filling in the centre, spread it along the radius and gently fold the pancake from both sides. Sprinkle a little more ghee or vegetable oil. Serve at once with *sambhar* and coconut chutney (p. 22).

CHEF'S NOTE

You can refrigerate the leftover batter in an airtight container for up to 3 weeks.

NON-VEGETARIAN

AAMLETTE

Spicy omelette

• Ingredients •

→ 6 eggs

→ Salt, to taste

→ Black pepper (*kali mirch*) powder, to taste

→ Red chilli powder, to taste

→ 3–4 Tbsp (45–60 ml) vegetable oil

→ 1 Tbsp (15 g) green chillies, chopped

→ 1 cup (170 g) onions, chopped

• Method •

1 In a large bowl, break the eggs and beat till frothy. Mix in the salt, black pepper powder and red chilli powder.

2 In a skillet over medium heat, heat 1 Tbsp oil.

3 Pour in half the egg mixture, reduce heat and sprinkle half the green chillies and onions.

4 As the mixture dries, slowly turn it over. Cook for another minute. Remove and cut into 3 pieces. Repeat till all the egg mixture is used up.

5 Serve while still hot with chilli or tomato sauce, if desired.

MUTTON SEEKH KEBAB

Thin meat slices roasted on skewers

• Ingredients •

- → 2 lb, 3 oz (1 kg) mutton, minced
- → 2 eggs, whisked
- → 2 tsp ground cumin (*jeera*)
- → ½ tsp ground white pepper
- → 1 tsp red chilli powder
- → 1 tsp coriander (*dhaniya*) powder
- → Salt, to taste
- → 3 Tbsp (45 g) cashew paste

- → 4 tsp ginger-garlic (*adrak-lasan*) paste
- → 4 tsp onion paste
- → 1 tsp garam masala
- → Pinch saffron (*kesar*) threads, soaked in 2 Tbsp (30 ml) warm milk
- → 5 Tbsp (5 g) green coriander (*hara dhaniya*) leaves, finely chopped
- → ½ cup (120 g) processed cheese, grated

• Method •

1 In a large bowl, combine the minced mutton, eggs, cumin, coriander powder, red chilli powder, white pepper, salt, cashew paste, ginger garlic paste, onion paste, garam masala, saffron, coriander leaves, and cheese. Mix well. Set aside for 30 minutes.

2 Shape the mince mixture along the length of the skewers to shape into kebabs.

3 Preheat the oven to 180°C (350°F).

4 Place the skewered kebabs on a baking sheet. Roast for 20–25 minutes.

5 Remove from skewers and serve hot.

TANDOORI CHICKEN

The much-loved, street-style barbecued chicken

• Ingredients •

→ 6 Tbsp (90 g) yoghurt (*dahi*)

→ 2 tsp ginger-garlic (*adrak-lasan*) paste

→ 1 tsp green chilli paste

→ 1 tsp red chilli powder

→ 2 tsp ground coriander (*dhaniya*)

→ 1 tsp garam masala

→ 1 Tbsp (10 g) tandoori masala (available at grocery stores)

→ 1 tsp ground cumin (*jeera*)

→ Salt, to taste

→ 1 whole chicken, cut into 8 pieces

→ Oil, for basting

→ 1 Tbsp (10 g) chaat masala

→ 1 tsp lemon juice

• Method •

1 In a medium-size bowl, combine the yoghurt, ginger-garlic paste, green chilli paste, red chilli powder, coriander, garam masala, tandoori masala, and cumin. Season to taste with salt. Whisk together to form a thick marinade.

2 Rub the marinade over the chicken and refrigerate for 3–4 hours.

3 Preheat the oven to 180°C (350°F).

4 Grill the pieces for 25–30 minutes.

5 Halfway, remove the chicken from the oven and baste it with oil.

6 Once cooked, sprinkle chaat masala and lemon juice and serve hot.

AMRITSARI MACCHI

Spicy fried fish fillet

• Ingredients •

→ 2 sole fillets

→ Juice of 1 lemon

→ 1 Tbsp (15 g) ginger-garlic (*adrak-lasan*) paste

→ 1 tsp carom (*ajwain*) seeds

→ 1 tsp red chilli powder

→ 1 tsp ground turmeric (*haldi*)

→ Pinch ground asafoetida (*hing*)

→ 1 Tbsp (8 g) chickpea flour (*besan*)

→ 1 tsp rice flour

→ Salt, to taste

→ Vegetable oil, for frying

→ 1 Tbsp (10 g) chaat masala

• Method •

1 In a medium-size bowl, combine the fish, lemon juice, ginger-garlic paste, carom seeds, red chilli powder, turmeric, asafoetida, chickpea flour, and rice flour. Season to taste with salt and marinade the fish for 10 minutes.

2 In a deep skillet over medium heat, heat the vegetable oil for frying.

3 Carefully add the fish to the hot oil and deep-fry until golden on both sides.

4 Sprinkle with the chaat masala before serving.

MURGI MINCED CUTLETS

Melt-in-your-mouth chicken croquettes

· Ingredients ·

- → 1 cup (240 g) chicken, minced

- → 1 cup (225 g) potatoes, mashed

- → 3 Tbsp (45 ml) heavy cream

- → 3 Tbsp (45 g) Cheddar cheese, grated

- → 2 green chillies, minced

- → 1 Tbsp (15 g) ginger-garlic (*adrak-lasan*) paste

- → ½ cup (63 g) refined flour (*maida*)

- → Salt, to taste

- → Freshly ground black pepper (*kali mirch*), to taste

- → ½ cup (58 g) bread crumbs

- → 2 eggs, whisked

- → Vegetable oil, for deep-frying

· Method ·

1 In a medium-size bowl, mix together the chicken, mashed potatoes, cream, cheese, green chillies, ginger-garlic paste, flour, salt, and pepper. Divide the mixture equally into 10 small portions. Shape each portion into a croquette.

2 Place the bread crumbs in a shallow bowl.

3 Dip the croquettes in the whisked eggs and then coat them with bread crumbs. Repeat until all are coated.

4 In a deep skillet over medium-high heat, heat the vegetable oil for deep-frying.

5 A few at a time, carefully add the croquettes to the hot oil and deep-fry until golden brown and crisp. Transfer to paper towels to drain.

6 Serve hot with your favourite chutneys.

MANGSHO GHUGNI

Lamb with chickpeas

• Ingredients •

- ½ cup (100 g) chickpeas (*kabuli chana*)
- 5 Tbsp (75 ml) vegetable oil
- ¼ cup (43 g) onions, chopped
- 1 tsp ginger paste
- 1 tsp garlic paste
- ¼ cup (60 g) tomatoes, chopped
- 1 cup (200 g) lamb pieces, boneless

- ½ tsp red chilli powder
- ½ tsp ground coriander (*dhaniya*)
- ½ tsp ground cumin (*jeera*)
- 2½ cups (600 ml) water, plus more for soaking chickpeas
- Salt, to taste
- 1 Tbsp (1 g) green coriander (*hara dhaniya*) leaves, finely chopped

• Method •

1 Soak the chickpeas in water overnight. Drain and discard water. In a saucepan over medium heat, boil the chickpeas in 1½ cups water until soft. Without draining, set aside.

2 In a skillet over low-medium heat, heat the vegetable oil. Add the onions, ginger paste, garlic paste, tomatoes, and lamb. Mix well.

3 Add the red chilli powder, coriander, cumin, and 1 cup of water. Season to taste with salt. Cook until the lamb is tender.

4 Add the boiled chickpeas along with the water in which they were boiled. Bring the mixture to a boil. Remove from the heat and serve hot, garnished with green coriander.

LUKMI
Stuffed flour rectangles

• Ingredients •

For the filling:

→ 2 Tbsp (30 ml) vegetable oil

→ 2 Tbsp (20 g) onions, chopped

→ 2 tsp garlic paste

→ 2 tsp ginger paste

→ 1½ cups (360 g) lamb, minced

→ ½ tsp turmeric (*haldi*) powder

→ 2 Tbsp (2 g) green coriander (*hara dhaniya*), chopped

→ 1 medium-size green chilli, chopped

→ 1 tsp coriander (*dhaniya*) powder

→ Salt, to taste

→ Red chilli powder, to taste

→ Vegetable oil, for deep-frying

For the dough:

→ 2 cups (250 g) refined flour (*maida*)

→ Salt, to taste

→ 1 Tbsp (15 g) yoghurt (*dahi*)

→ 2 Tbsp (15 g or 15 ml) ghee or vegetable oil

• Method •

1 For the filling: In a wok over low-medium heat, heat the oil. Add the onions and sauté until brown. Add garlic and ginger pastes. Add the lamb mince and cook for 10 minutes. Add the rest of the ingredients and cook for 5 minutes more. Keep the filling aside to cool.

2 For the dough: In a large bowl, mix the flour and salt together. Add the yoghurt, ghee or oil, and sufficient water to make a stiff dough. Divide the dough into equal parts and shape into balls. Then roll them out in strips 3–4 in. long and about 2 in. wide. Place 1 Tbsp of the filling in the centre of each rectangle and fold it so it is approximately 2 in. by 1.5 in. Press and seal the edges after wetting them a bit.

3 In a wok over medium heat, heat the oil. Working in batches, fry the rectangles on medium heat until cooked. Remove with a slotted spoon and drain on paper towels.

EGG BANJO
Masala omelette burger

• Ingredients •

- 2 eggs
- ¼ cup (4 g) green coriander (*hara dhaniya*) leaves, finely chopped
- 1 tsp cumin (*jeera*) seeds
- 1 tsp ginger, julienned, peeled
- 1 tsp red chilli powder
- 1 medium-size green chilli, finely chopped

- Salt, to taste
- 2 tsp olive oil
- 1 Tbsp (15 g) butter
- 2 burger buns, split
- ½ cup (120 g) onions, sliced
- 1 medium-size tomato, sliced
- 1 Tbsp (20 g) ketchup

• Method •

1 In a small bowl, whisk the eggs, coriander, cumin seeds, ginger, red chilli powder, and green chilli. Season to taste with salt.

2 In a small skillet over medium heat, heat the olive oil.

3 Pour half the egg batter into the skillet and spread it evenly. Cook on both sides until golden brown.

Remove and set aside. Repeat with the remaining egg batter.

4 Butter one half of each bun and place an omelette on top of each. Layer with onion and tomato slices.

5 Apply ketchup to the other halves of the buns and close the sandwiches. Cut the burgers in half and serve with your favourite chutneys.

SERVES 2-4

MAACHER CHOP
Fried fish and potato cakes

• Ingredients •

- → 1 tsp ghee
- → 1¼ cups (300 g) carp (*rohu*) or any other white-fleshed fish, boiled, deboned
- → 1 cup (225 g) potatoes, boiled, peeled, mashed
- → 1 tsp milk
- → ½ tsp salt, plus more to taste
- → 2 green chillies, chopped
- → 1 tsp ginger paste
- → 1 tsp lemon juice
- → 1 egg, white only
- → Vegetable oil, for deep-frying
- → Bread crumbs, to coat

• Method •

1 In a skillet over medium-high heat, heat the ghee.

2 Add the fish, potatoes, and milk.

3 Sauté for a few minutes, stirring continuously. Remove from the heat.

4 Add salt to taste, green chillies, ginger paste, and lemon juice. Mix well.

5 In a medium-size bowl, whisk the egg white with ½ tsp of salt. Set aside.

6 Divide the fish mixture equally into 6–8 small balls.

7 In a wok over high heat, heat the vegetable oil for deep-frying.

8 Dip the balls in the whisked egg white and roll in bread crumbs. Working in batches, carefully put the balls in hot oil. Deep-fry until golden brown. Transfer to paper towels to drain. Serve hot.

MANGSHO CUTLET

Bengali-style lamb cutlets

• Ingredients •

- → 2 white bread slices
- → 1 lb, 2 oz (500 g) lamb, minced
- → ½ tsp garam masala
- → 1 medium-size onion, finely chopped
- → 4 green chillies, finely chopped

- → 1 tsp fresh mint (*pudina*) leaves
- → Salt, to taste
- → 8 eggs, whisked
- → ½ cup (58 g) bread crumbs
- → ¼ cup (60 g) ghee

• Method •

1 Dip the bread slices in water, soaking them well. Remove and squeeze out all the water.

2 In a medium-size bowl, combine the lamb mince, bread slices, garam masala, onion, green chillies, and mint leaves. Season to taste with salt. Set aside for 1 hour.

3 Divide the mixture into 10 portions; shape each portion into flat cutlets. Set aside on a tray.

4 In a small bowl, whisk together the eggs with salt.

5 Set out the bread crumbs on a tray or shallow dish.

6 In a wok over medium-high heat, heat the ghee.

7 Dip the cutlets in the egg mixture, then roll in the bread crumbs.

8 Fry each cutlet in the wok until golden brown. Transfer to paper towels to drain and serve.

CHINGRI CUTLET

Deep-fried prawn cutlet

• Ingredients •

→ 6 prawns, cleaned

→ 1 egg

→ 1 medium-size onion, ground to a fine paste

→ 1 Tbsp (15 g) garlic paste

→ 2 tsp red chilli powder

→ 1 tsp garam masala

→ Salt, to taste

→ Vegetable oil, for frying

→ 1 cup (120 g) chickpea flour (*besan*)

→ 1 cup (115 g) bread crumbs

• Method •

1 Place the prawns between two sheets of plastic wrap and flatten with a meat pounder.

2 In a small bowl, stir together the egg, onion paste, garlic paste, red chilli powder, and garam masala. Season to taste with salt. Stir well and add the prawns. Stir again to combine. Refrigerate to marinade for 1 hour.

3 In a deep skillet over low-medium heat, heat the vegetable oil for frying.

4 In a shallow bowl, combine the chickpea flour and bread crumbs. Season to taste with salt. Dip the marinaded prawns in the flour–bread crumb mixture.

5 Carefully add the prawns to the hot oil and deep-fry until golden.

6 Serve hot.

SHAMMI KEBAB
Pan-fried minced-meat cakes

• Ingredients •

→ 5 whole cloves (*laung*)

→ 5 green cardamom (*choti elaichi*) pods

→ 4 dried red chillies (*sookhi lal mirch*)

→ 3 black cardamom (*badi elaichi*) pods

→ 2 whole mace

→ 1 in. cinnamon stick

→ ¼ tsp ground nutmeg

→ 2 Tbsp (12 g) cumin (*jeera*) seeds

→ 1 Tbsp (15 g) peppercorns (*sabut kali mirch*)

→ 1 Tbsp (9 g) poppy seeds (*khus khus*)

→ 1 cup (250 g) coconut flesh, dry-roasted

→ 2 in. ginger, grated, peeled

→ 8 garlic cloves, minced

→ 5 Tbsp (75 g) raw papaya, grated

→ 1 medium-size onion, sliced, fried

→ ¾ cup (90 g) chickpea flour (*besan*), toasted

→ ½ cup (120 g) yoghurt (*dahi*)

→ 2 lb, 3 oz (1 kg) lamb or beef, minced

→ 1 Tbsp (15 g) salt

→ Green chillies, to taste, chopped

→ Fresh mint (*pudina*) leaves, chopped

• Method •

1 Preheat a griddle over low-medium heat. On the hot griddle, combine the cloves, green cardamom pods, dried red chillies, black cardamom pods, mace, cinnamon stick, nutmeg, cumin seeds, peppercorns, poppy seeds, and coconut. Dry-roast until fragrant, stirring frequently. Transfer to a food processor or spice grinder and process until ground. Transfer to a medium-size bowl to cool.

2 To the bowl, add the ginger, garlic, papaya, fried onion, chickpea flour, yoghurt, and minced meat.

Season to taste with salt, green chillies, and mint. Mix well to combine all the ingredients. Divide the mixture into 20–25 small portions. With greased palms, shape each into a flat cake.

3 Wipe out the griddle, if needed, and place it over medium-high heat and add just a little ghee to melt.

4 Working in batches, pan-fry the cakes until golden brown on both sides. Remove and repeat until all are fried, adding more ghee as needed. Serve hot.

MOMO

A popular dim-sum-like dumpling

• Ingredients •

For the momo sheets:

→ 2 cups (250 g) refined flour (*maida*)

→ 1 tsp salt

→ ½ tsp baking powder

→ Water, to knead

For the filling:

→ 2 Tbsp (30 ml) vegetable oil

→ 2 Tbsp (30 g) garlic, grated

→ 1 Tbsp (8 g) ginger, chopped

→ 1 small onion, finely chopped

→ 1 cup (240 g) mutton (can also use chicken, pork or beef), cleaned, minced, boiled

→ ½ tsp ground turmeric (*haldi*)

→ 2 carrots, grated

→ 1 Tbsp (15 ml) soy sauce

→ 1 tsp vinegar

→ Salt, to taste

→ Freshly ground black pepper (*kali mirch*), to taste

• Method •

1 For the momo sheets: In a bowl, mix all the ingredients listed. Knead into a soft dough and set aside.

2 For the filling: In a skillet over medium-high heat, heat the vegetable oil.

3 Add garlic, ginger, and onion. Fry for 5 minutes.

4 Add the boiled mince. Stir in the turmeric, carrots, soy sauce and vinegar. Season to taste with salt and black pepper. Cook for 5 minutes.

5 Roll the dough out into thin circular discs (about the size of your palm). Place a spoonful of the filling in the centre.

6 Bring the edges together towards the centre and pinch it with your fingertips to create small parcels, or fold into half and stick the edges together like a crescent. Moisten your hands with water to ensure the dough sticks together.

7 In a large vessel over high heat, bring water to a boil. Place the parcels on a greased plate or a steamer and put it on top of the boiling water.

8 Steam the momos for 7–8 minutes, or until done. Serve hot with hot sauce, if desired.

CHILLI CHICKEN

A hint of the Chinese influence on Kolkata

• Ingredients •

→ ¼ cup (32 g) cornstarch

→ 1 egg

→ 1 tsp garlic powder

→ Salt, to taste

→ Freshly ground black pepper (*kali mirch*), to taste

→ 1 cup (240 g) chicken, boneless, cubed

→ Vegetable oil, for frying

→ 1 Tbsp (15 g) minced garlic

→ 2 green chillies, minced

→ ½ cup (85 g) onions, diced

→ ½ cup (75 g) green bell peppers, diced

→ 3 Tbsp (45 ml) tomato sauce

→ 1 Tbsp (15 ml) chilli sauce

→ 2 tsp white vinegar

→ 2 tsp soy sauce

→ ¼ cup (15 g) spring onions, finely chopped

→ 2 tsp white sesame (*safed til*) seeds

· Method ·

1 In a medium-size bowl, whisk the cornstarch, egg, and garlic powder. Season to taste with salt and pepper.

2 Add the chicken and stir well to coat.

3 Refrigerate to marinade for 2 hours.

4 In a deep skillet over medium heat, heat the vegetable oil for frying.

5 Carefully add the chicken to the hot oil and deep-fry until golden. Remove and set aside.

6 In another skillet over low-medium heat, heat some vegetable oil.

7 Add the garlic and green chillies. Sauté for 1 minute.

8 Add the onions and green bell peppers. Stir-fry for 4–5 minutes.

9 Stir in the tomato sauce, chilli sauce, vinegar, and soy sauce. Season to taste with salt and pepper.

10 Finish by adding the chicken cubes and spring onions.

11 Garnish with sesame seeds and serve hot.

CHICKEN KATHI ROLL

Barbecued chicken rolled in an egg-coated paratha

• Ingredients •

For the filling:

→ 1 lb, 2 oz (500 g) chicken, boneless, cut into 2 in. pieces

→ 2 Tbsp (20 g) onions, chopped

→ 1 Tbsp (15 g) garlic paste

→ 1 Tbsp (15 g) ginger paste

→ 1 Tbsp (6 g) coriander (*dhaniya*) powder

→ ½ tsp turmeric (*haldi*) powder

→ 1 tsp garam masala

→ 2 green chillies, chopped

→ Juice of 1 lemon

→ Salt, to taste

For the salad filling:

→ 2 large onions, finely sliced

→ 1 cup (16 g) green coriander (*hara dhaniya*), finely chopped

→ 6 green chillies, finely chopped

→ 4 medium-size tomatoes, chopped, optional

For the flatbread (paratha):

→ 3 cups (375 g) refined flour (*maida*)

→ Salt, to taste

→ 3 Tbsp (45 ml) vegetable oil, plus more for frying

→ Water, to knead

→ Eggs

• Method •

1 For the filling: Preheat the oven to 180°C (350°F).

2 In a large bowl, mix all the ingredients and marinade for 2 hours. Skewer the kebabs and cook in the oven for 20 minutes or till done. (The kebabs can also be fried.)

3 For the salad filling: In a bowl, mix all the ingredients together and set aside.

4 For the flatbread (paratha): In a large bowl, sieve the salt and refined flour and rub in the oil. Using sufficient water, knead gently to form a soft dough. Cover and set aside for 30 minutes.

5 Divide the dough equally into 12 balls. Roll out each ball in approximately 7 or 8 in. discs.

6 Heat a griddle or a thick-bottomed frying pan and lay one disc on it. When one side is slightly cooked, turn and cook the other side similarly. Add 1 Tbsp oil on each side, spread evenly and lightly fry both sides. Break an egg over the paratha and spread it evenly. Pour a little oil on the egg and the sides. When the egg is done, remove and set aside. Make similar parathas with the remaining batter and set aside.

7 To assemble the kathi, spread a sheet of greaseproof paper; put a paratha on it, topped with chicken pieces and salad filling. Roll together and serve hot with your favourite chutneys, if desired.

CHEF'S NOTE

You can use lamb or cottage cheese instead of chicken.

DESSERTS

GAJAR KA HALWA

Shredded carrot pudding

• Ingredients •

→ 2 lb, 3 oz (1 kg) carrots, washed, peeled, shredded

→ 2½ cups (600 ml) milk

→ 1 tsp ground green cardamom (*choti elaichi*), divided

→ ½ cup (100 g) sugar

→ ½ cup (113 g) brown sugar

→ 4 Tbsp (60 g) ghee

→ ⅓ cup (30 g) almonds, slivered

→ ⅛ cup (25 g) raisins (*kishmish*)

→ ⅓ cup (40 g) walnuts, chopped

→ ½ tsp ground cloves (*laung*)

→ ½ tsp ground nutmeg

→ ½ tsp ground cinnamon

• Method •

1 In a pan over medium-high heat, boil the shredded carrots with the milk. Simmer and cook for 20–25 minutes, stirring continuously until the liquid evaporates.

2 Add half the ground cardamom, brown sugar, and regular sugar. Stir continuously for 10–12 minutes. Remove and set the mixture aside.

3 In a wok over medium heat, heat the ghee.

4 Fry the slivered almonds until golden.

5 Add the prepared carrot mixture, raisins, walnuts, cloves, nutmeg, and cinnamon. Cook until the mixture begins to separate from the sides and caramelizes into a deep red colour.

KULFI FALOODA

Street-style ice cream with summery flavours

• Ingredients •

→ 1 cup (240 ml) full-fat milk

→ 1 cup (240 ml) heavy cream

→ 1 Tbsp (8 g) cornflour

→ ½ cup (100 g) powdered sugar

→ 1 tsp saffron (*kesar*) threads

→ 3 Tbsp (45 g) whole-milk fudge (*khoya*)

→ 2 Tbsp (30 g) assorted fruits, dried, sliced

→ 1 cup (200 g) vermicelli (*seviyan*),

soaked in water for 10–15 minutes, drained

→ 5 tsp rose syrup

→ 2 tsp saffron syrup, optional

→ ½ cup (88 g) basil seeds (*sabja*) or chia seeds, soaked in water for 10–12 minutes or until sprouted

→ 1 Tbsp (9 g) assorted nuts, finely chopped

→ 1 silver leaf (*warq*), for garnishing, optional

• Method •

1 In a medium-size saucepan over medium-high heat, bring the milk to a rolling boil. Add the cream and cornflour. Stir well to combine.

2 Add the powdered sugar, saffron threads, and whole-milk fudge. Add the sliced dried fruits. Mix well. Bring the milk to another boil. Remove from the heat and set aside to cool.

3 Transfer to plastic kulfi moulds and freeze until set. Once set, bring them out of the freezer. In a tall glass, layer one-fifth of the vermicelli and place one piece of kulfi on top. Drizzle 1 tsp of rose syrup and one-fifth of the saffron syrup (if using) on top. Add 1½ tsp of basil seeds or chia seeds on top.

4 Garnish with nuts and silver leaf (if using) and serve immediately.

JALEBI

A light and delicious energy-giving sweet

• Ingredients •

→ 6 Tbsp (60 g) refined flour (*maida*)

→ 2 Tbsp (15 g) chickpea flour (*besan*)

→ 2 Tbsp (30 g) yoghurt (*dahi*)

→ 1 Tbsp (15 ml) vegetable oil, plus more for deep-frying

→ 3¾ cup (900 ml) water

→ 1¾ cups (350 g) sugar

• Method •

1 Mix the refined flour, chickpea flour, yoghurt, oil and ¾ cup water together and let it ferment overnight.

2 Make the syrup with 3 cups of water and sugar till a one-string consistency is achieved. Set aside.

3 Heat the oil for deep-frying in a flat pan. Beat flour mixture thoroughly and pack it in a plastic bag. Cut a small hole in one corner and slowly squeeze the bag over the hot oil. Try to make 2 in. whirls starting from the outer ring and ending at the centre. Fry till both sides are crisp. To turn over, use a steel or bamboo skewer. Remove gently with tongs and drain.

4 Soak the whirls in the syrup for about 4 minutes and then take them out. Serve hot.

GULAB JAMUN

Milk-based dessert in sugar syrup

• Ingredients •

For the dumplings:

→ 2 cups (250 g) full-cream milk powder

→ 1 cup (125 g) refined flour (*maida*)

→ ½ cup (85 g) semolina (*suji*), fine

→ Thick cream, to knead

→ Vegetable oil, for deep-frying

For the sugar syrup:

→ 2¼ cups (450 g) sugar

→ 3 cups (720 ml) water

→ 3 tsp rose water

• Method •

1 For the dumplings: In a bowl, mix all the ingredients and knead with a light touch to form a soft dough. Divide the mixture into 25 portions and shape them into balls.

2 For the sugar syrup: In a saucepan over low-medium heat, boil the water and sugar till the sugar dissolves completely and the syrup is of one-string consistency when tested between the thumb and index finger. When cool, stir in rose water.

3 In a wok over medium heat, heat the oil. Carefully lower a few balls, one at a time, gently shaking the oil constantly so that they become uniformly brown. Remove the balls and immerse them in sugar syrup. Repeat until all the balls are fried. Soak the dumplings for an hour in the syrup.

4 Serve warm.

SHAHI TUKDA

Rich bread dessert sprinkled with dry fruits

• Ingredients •

→ 4 bread slices cut into triangles, with the crust removed

→ 2 tsp ghee

→ 1½ cups (360 ml) milk, full-cream

→ 4 Tbsp (50 g) sugar

→ A few strands saffron (*kesar*), dissolved in 2 Tbsp (30 ml) of hot water

→ 10 almonds, blanched, peeled, sliced

→ 10 raisins (*kishmish*), soaked in hot water for 15 minutes

• Method •

1 Heat the oil and fry the bread triangles till golden. Remove with a slotted spoon and drain on paper towels. Set aside.

2 Heat the ghee in a large frying pan. Add the fried slices of bread. Pour the milk over them and sprinkle the sugar. Turn the slices over carefully, taking care that they do not break. Cook till the milk thickens and changes colour, stirring gently.

3 Remove from heat, add the saffron and serve chilled, sprinkled with almonds and raisins.

BESAN LADOO

Sweet chickpea flour balls

• Ingredients •

→ ½ cup (120 g) ghee

→ 2 cups (240 g) chickpea flour (*besan*)

→ ½ cup (100 g) powdered sugar

→ 2 Tbsp (10 g) almond powder

→ 1 tsp ground green cardamom (*choti elaichi*)

• Method •

1 In a heavy-bottomed skillet over medium heat, heat the ghee.

2 Add the chickpea flour. Stir-fry for 2–3 minutes until the flour turns dark brown. Remove from the heat.

3 Stir in the sugar, almond powder, and cardamom. Continue to mix until the sugar dissolves completely.

4 Divide the mixture equally into 12 small portions. Roll each into a small ball and store in an airtight container for up to a week

PAYASAM
Rice pudding with poppy seeds and jaggery

• Ingredients •

→ 1½ cups (300 g) rice

→ 3 Tbsp (27 g) poppy seeds (*khus khus*)

→ 1 cup (85 g) unsweetened coconut, grated, dried

→ 1 cup (240 ml) milk

→ ½ cup (120 g) jaggery (*gur*; unrefined cane sugar, grated)

→ Pinch ground green cardamom (*choti elaichi*)

• Method •

1 In a medium-size bowl, combine the rice and poppy seeds, with enough water to cover, for 5 hours.

2 Drain and transfer to a blender. Add the coconut. Blend the mixture into a thick paste.

3 Transfer to a heavy-bottomed pot and place it over low-medium heat on the stove. Pour in the milk. Mix well. Bring to a simmer and cook until the milk begins to bubble.

4 Add the jaggery. Cook, stirring, until it dissolves completely. Keep stirring until the mixture has a porridge-like consistency. Remove from the heat. Sprinkle with cardamom and serve.

GAJAK

Sweet sesame snack, best enjoyed in winter

· Ingredients ·

- → 3 Tbsp (45 g) ghee, plus more for preparing the baking sheet

- → ¾ cup (108 g) white sesame (*safed til*) seeds

- → 1 cup (200 g) sugar

- → 3 Tbsp (45 ml) water

- → ¼ cup (36 g) cashews, coarsely chopped

- → ¼ cup (36 g) peanuts, coarsely chopped

- → 1 Tbsp (2 g) dried food-grade rose petals

· Method ·

1 Line a baking sheet with parchment paper and grease it with ghee. Set aside.

2 In a heavy-bottomed saucepan over low heat, roast the sesame seeds until slightly toasted. Remove from the heat and transfer the seeds to a bowl. Set aside.

3 Return the pan to the heat and melt the ghee.

4 Add the sugar and water. Allow it to bubble until it turns into a thick syrup. Remove from the heat and stir in the toasted sesame seeds, cashews, peanuts, and rose petals. Using a flat spatula, spread the mixture evenly on the prepared sheet.

5 While the mixture is still warm and soft, cut it into six 1 in. squares and allow it to set for 1 hour. Once it hardens, remove from the tray and store in airtight jars.

MISHTI DOI

Sweet yoghurt — a fitting end to a good Bengali meal

• Ingredients •

→ 11 cups (2.6 L) full-cream milk

→ 1 cup (200 g) sugar

→ 2 Tbsp (30 g) yoghurt (*dahi*)

• Method •

1 In a saucepan over low heat, cook the milk until it is reduced to 1.2 L.

2 Boil the milk, and then add the sugar. Boil until the sugar dissolves completely. Set aside to cool. The mixture should be lukewarm.

3 Spread the yoghurt in a stone, ceramic or earthen pot. Pour a cup of hot milk and mix quickly. Now pour in the remaining milk, stir once, then cover and set aside in a closed, warm place to set. This takes 12-15 hours, depending on the weather.

4 If you want a nice, frothy top, pour the last bit of the milk from a little height. After the yoghurt is set, put it in the refrigerator for a couple of hours before serving. The yoghurt will keep for 4-5 days.

DRINKS

NIMBU PANI

Lemonade with medicinal qualities

• Ingredients •

- ¾ cup (180 ml) fresh lemon juice

- ⅓ cup (43 g) fresh mint (*pudina*) leaves, plus sprigs for garnish

- ⅓ cup (67 g) sugar

- ½ tsp grated black salt (*kala namak*), optional

- ½ tsp kosher salt

- ¼ tsp dried mango powder (*amchoor*)

- ¼ tsp freshly ground black pepper (*kali mirch*)

- ¼ tsp ground cumin (*jeera*)

- 4 cups (960 ml) soda or water, chilled

- Lemon slices, for serving

• Method •

1 In a blender, combine the lemon juice, mint leaves, sugar, black salt (if using), kosher salt, dried mango powder, pepper, and cumin. Blend until smooth. Pour into a pitcher and top with soda or water.

2 Garnish with lime slices and mint sprigs.

MEETHI LASSI

SERVES 2

Sweet yoghurt drink

• Ingredients •

→ 2 cups (480 g) chilled yoghurt (*dahi*)

→ 1 Tbsp (13 g) powdered sugar

→ Pinch salt

→ 1 cup (140 g) crushed ice

• Method •

1 In a small bowl, whisk the yoghurt, powdered sugar, and salt. Add crushed ice.

2 Serve in tall glasses garnished with any fruit, if desired.

CHEF'S NOTE

To make namkeen lassi (savoury lassi), add 1 tsp cumin seeds, roasted and powdered, ¼ tsp salt, and ¼ tsp rock salt instead of powdered sugar.

MASALA CHAI

Flavoured tea

· Ingredients ·

→ 6 cups (1.4 L) water

→ 4 tsp tea leaves or tea dust

→ 1 tsp ginger, roughly chopped

→ 2 green cardamom (*choti elaichi*) pods, powdered

→ ½ cup (120 ml) milk

→ Sugar, to taste, optional

· Method ·

1 In a saucepan, boil the water, tea leaves or tea dust, ginger and green cardamom powder together for 3 minutes. Add the milk and sugar, if using, and boil for another 2 minutes.

2 Strain through a fine wire-mesh strainer and serve at once.

MANGO JAL JEERA

Refreshing raw mango drink

• Ingredients •

- → 1 cup (175 g) raw mango (*kairi*), finely chopped
- → ¼ cup (4 g) green coriander (*hara dhaniya*) leaves, finely chopped
- → ¼ cup (16 g) fresh mint (*pudina*) leaves, finely chopped
- → 2 Tbsp (25 g) sugar

- → 1 tsp ground cumin (*jeera*)
- → 1 tsp black salt (*kala namak*)
- → Salt, to taste
- → Cold water, as needed
- → Ice, as needed

• Method •

1 In a blender, combine all the ingredients and blend until smooth. Add cold water to adjust the consistency.

2 Strain and transfer the mixture into tall glasses. Add ice or more cold water and stir well before serving.

CHEF'S NOTE

It is recommended to keep the mixture in the refrigerator for one day to let all the flavours blend in.

AAM KA PANNA

Raw mango summer drink

• Ingredients •

→ 2 medium-size raw mangoes

→ 4 cups (960 ml) water

→ 3 Tbsp (38 g) sugar

→ 1 tsp black salt (*kala namak*)

→ 1 tsp ground cumin (*jeera*)

• Method •

1 Preheat the oven to 180°C (350°F).

2 Make four slits in the mangoes lengthwise and place them on a baking sheet. Bake for 40 minutes.

3 Press the charred mango skin to extract the pulp into a large bowl.

4 Stir in the water, mixing well.

5 Add the sugar, black salt, and cumin. Whisk to combine. Refrigerate and serve chilled.

COCONUT SHERBET

Coconut crush

• Ingredients •

→ 2 cups (480 ml) coconut water

→ ½ cup (125 g) coconut flesh

→ ½ cup (120 ml) water

→ Sugar, to taste

• Method •

1 In a blender, blitz all the ingredients together into a thick shake.

2 Transfer into two tall glasses and serve chilled.

FILTER COFFEE

The distinctive aroma of South Indian coffee is unforgettable

• Ingredients •

→ 1 Tbsp (20 g) South Indian coffee beans

→ ½ cup (120 ml) boiling water

→ 2-3 cups (480-720 ml) milk

→ Sugar, to taste

• Method •

1 In a frying pan over low-medium heat, dry-roast the coffee beans for a minute or two.

2 Transfer the roasted coffee beans to a food processor and grind to a fine powder.

3 Put the powder in the upper chamber of a coffee filter. Add the boiling water. Cover and allow the coffee to percolate to the bottom container of the filter.

4 In a saucepan, bring the milk to a boil.

5 Divide the strained coffee into four tumblers. Pour equal portions of hot milk into each. Holding an empty tumbler in the left hand, pour the entire coffee-milk mixture into it, ensuring that you pour from a height to make it frothy. Sugar may be added to the milk, if desired. Serve at once.